Good Housekeeping

A War Bride's Guide to the U.S.A.

Good Housekeeping

A War Bride's Guide to the U.S.A.

COLLINS & BROWN

First published in United Kingdom in 2006 by
Collins & Brown Limited
151 Freston Road
London W10 6TH

An imprint of Anova Books Company Ltd.

The Good Housekeeping website address is
www.goodhousekeeping.co.uk

1 2 3 4 5 6 7 8 9

ISBN 1-84340-382-X

A catalogue record for this book is available from the British Library.

Printed and bound by MPG Books Ltd, Bodmin, Cornwall

This book can be ordered direct from the publisher. Contact the
marketing department, but try your bookshop first.

www.anovabooks.com

∽ CONTENTS ∽

By the end of World War II, over 100,000 British women had married American servicemen. But marrying a GI was one thing, getting to the United States was another. Strict US immigration quotas and lack of transport meant that most of these women, many with babies or young children, were unable to join their husbands in the United States.

In October 1945, a crowd of women picketed the US Embassy shouting, 'We want our husbands! We want ships!' Two months later, on December 29th, the US Congress passed the War Bride's Act, which allowed entry to the United States of alien wives and minor children of American citizens who had been in active service during the war by granting them special status, regardless of the immigration quotas. Soon afterwards, the War Department began Operation *Diaper Run*, a sealift to reunite husbands, wives and children in America. Thirty ships were commandeered to bring the women over. On January 26th 1946, the first 'war bride' ship, the *S.S. Argentina*, left Southampton carrying 452 war brides and their children, arriving in New York Harbor to the sounds of 'Here Comes the Bride' as they docked. Over the next weeks and months, the rest of the 100,000 women followed. Famous liners were also used for these crossing, including the *Queen Mary*, the *Queen Elizabeth* and the *Aquitania*.

Months before the War Bride's Act was finally passed and Operation *Diaper Run* had begun, *Good Housekeeping* had been educating British GI brides about their future home by publishing a small pamphlet called *A Bride's Guide to the*

U.S.A. Produced in June 1945 at the request of the US Office of War Information, it explained America and the Americans to the women before they said goodbye to their families and headed for a strange land. We have reproduced the text from the original pamphlet here along with poems, stories and features published in *Good Housekeeping* during the war years, which convey the warm and grateful attitude the British felt towards the United States by the end of the War.

But women were not only leaving Britain to move to America, many foreign women from around the world had married British servicemen during the war and were now coming to Britain to start a new life. In July 1945 *Good Housekeeping* printed an editorial urging GH readers to welcome these war brides to the country and to encourage them, if they were in need of any help or advice, to write to *Good Housekeeping*, just as hundreds of people still do, over sixty years later.

Louise

Louise Chunn
Editor-in-Chief
Good Housekeeping

⤜ A BRIDE'S GUIDE TO THE U.S.A. *⤜*

JUNE 1945

This pamplet provided British
war brides with vital information
on their new life in the America.

First prepared by British
GOOD HOUSEKEEPING MAGAZINE 1945
in conjunction with the
United States Office of War Information,
especially for British Brides of American Servicemen.

You have undertaken to become an American—just as millions of other people have done before you. Getting to know your adopted country will be an exciting adventure: the future is before you.

You have no doubt heard a good deal from your husband about the part of the United States where you will probably live, but you may still be wondering how you will get acquainted with people, what they will be like, and how you will manage your new home. This short guide cannot answer all your questions, but it may help you in making plans and in adjusting yourself to American ways of living.

One thing you will notice when you meet people in America is that most of them will start a conversation without much hesitation. But when you think it over, you may feel that they have not really said much to let you into their lives. And perhaps you felt too shy to say much in return. Actually, most Americans are shy, below the surface: they talk to cover it up and to make you feel their friendly intentions while they gradually get to know you. They won't be surprised if you are quiet. Smile, use your British habit of thanking people for everything, ask questions, and you will make people feel that you want to be friendly, too. In America it is good manners to praise anything you like, whether it is the food, the furniture, or the view from the window. Dress your smartest for first interviews and remember that, except in the smallest villages, lipstick is expected.

Listen, look around you, and take your time. Arm yourself with a few items of "small talk"—and any odd fact about your voyage, what you have seen, where you have been—to cover your thoughts while you look about. Ask questions about simple things—where to shop, what to buy, what to do for entertainment. Everyone likes to lend a hand to a stranger, and people who have done you a small favour and have been thanked with a smile will like you from then on.

Don't mind if at first you feel left out of some of the jokes that go by you in conversation. For one thing, most jokes in any country depend on some local topic or some peculiar twist of slang—no one expects a newcomer to get them. Just laugh and admit you don't.

A great deal of American written humour is like your own, but there are some kinds of spoken humour that you must learn to take calmly. Exaggeration, of course, you know about, and learning the American language includes recognising what is true and what is too absurd to believe. Kidding is perhaps harder to get used to, but you have to learn. It may consist of mimicking, to see if you "can take it". This variety is a subtle form of flattery, as it makes you the centre of attention and assumes that you can laugh at yourself, a quality that is much admired. Kidding also includes using insults as a sign of affection, but Americans, not being noticeably angelic, also use insults as a sign of anger. So the best thing to do is to take everything good-naturedly while you learn to understand the language. Later, you may learn to kid back, but don't try it till you know how.

The first lesson in "American" is the names of things. You will learn these quickly, as the Americans had to do in Britain. Some words you will already have learned from your husband, and there is a word list in the back that will help (see page 37). Use the American names, so as not to be misunderstood. You need not use American slang words that are offensive in English, but if they are harmless in America, don't be bothered by them. Change your pronunciation if it causes misunderstanding—otherwise don't. Keep your accent while you can; most English accents, especially when spoken by a girl, are regarded in America as charming.

American manners, as you know, are different in various ways, some of which you may not like. The Americans do not say "thank you" in as many situations as the British, and they often ask a question without begging pardon. It is good American, when thanked for a real favour, to say "you're welcome," "don't mention it," or "not at all". In American the word "sorry" is not as polite as "excuse me" or "I beg your pardon". Another thing is that Americans, as you have noticed, use first names easily on short acquaintance. These are all purely matters of form. A good rule is to watch how people talk to one another in your part of the country and not to be surprised or offended if they do the same to you.

As to table manners, your knife-and-fork system will seem strange to most Americans, but not bad-mannered. You can make a joke of trying to learn the American cut-and-switch system.

The other part of the American language that you need to learn is made up of facts about your part of the country and the life of the people around you. When you know something of the history of your locality, where the people came from, and what they are interested in, you will begin to know what they are talking about and why they say such curious things. This, of course, is a long job, but the sooner you start the sooner you will know your way around.

The best way to start is by reading, because in reading you can learn without being embarrassed by not knowing what to ask. Take a local newspaper and read the local news until names and local events make sense in your mind. Go to the Public Library and talk with the librarian, if it is a small library, or the reader's adviser if it is a big one. The best and most painless way to learn about your new home from books is to read novels about your state and region, and then about America. Some books are suggested in a list at the back. At the library look over the women's household magazines. Subscribe to one of them to help you on styles and ways of doing things about the house.

You may find yourself settled far from your husband's family and surrounded entirely by strangers. In a small town the neighbours will call on you and try to be friendly. Neighbourliness is highly valued in America. They will chat with you when you are hanging out the laundry or digging in your garden—which probably will have no hedges around it. Neighbours can be helpful and you can help them. If you are going shopping, ask your neighbour if you can get anything for her. In an emergency you can borrow a loaf of bread or a cup of sugar, but be sure to return them in kind as soon as possible. Borrowing and lending are friendly gestures if kept balanced and not overdone.

If your neighbours call on you, be sure to return the call in a few days. Then you can invite them over for an evening. Home entertainment is simple in America: people sit on the porch in summer or in the living-room in winter, six or eight together, talking or playing cards. Light refreshments are served about ten o'clock—coffee and cake, or iced ginger ale and sandwiches, perhaps some sweets or olives for decoration. Tea and scones might be a pleasant surprise. Since refreshments are so simple, people often "drop in" without formality. For dinner, of course, invitations are necessary.

In a big city you can be as lonely as in any strange city in Britain, and if you live in a flat you won't have any neighbours. People do not readily make friends with those who live above or below them.

But don't just sit down and die of home-sickness. There are ways of making friends even in New York or Chicago, but you have to be enterprising and self-reliant.

Wherever you find yourself, there are organisations that have open doors and expect strangers to come in on their own feet. The churches are still the principal ones. Then if you have belonged to the Red Cross or the Y.W.C.A. in Britain you will find its opposite number in America. The church or the library can tell you about welfare societies, Young People's societies, and other groups or clubs catering for hobbies, according to your tastes. These clubs and societies want enthusiastic members who will join and do some of the work. You may as well find some congenial organisation and work with it, for this is one of the best ways of making real friends.

If you have a hobby, you will probably find that others with the same hobby have formed an organisation where you will be welcome. If you like music, there may be a local orchestra or choral society—the music store can tell you. If you are keen on gardening, there is probably a Garden Club. If you like dramatics, there is likely to be a dramatics club that would be delighted to have you.

When you do get acquainted with people in a big city, entertaining will be somewhat different from what it is in a small town. People seldom "drop in," but couples often meet friends by arrangement for a dinner out, with a cinema, theatre, or dance afterward. Cocktail parties before dinner are more frequent. Sunday trips to the country or the beach are a good excuse for inviting new friends to go along.

Sports are especially good links with other people. Many towns and cities have public tennis courts; just go down and pick up a game. There are usually swimming-pools; the Y.W.C.A. can tell you about them. The Y.W.C.A. can also tell you about the local "keep fit" classes, dancing classes, social dances, and other affairs that you can attend by simply asking for admission.

Incidentally, when you see American sports or take part in them, don't expect them to go by British rules. American ball games, for instance, require a certain number of players, so an injured player, or even an uninjured one, can be replaced by a substitute. Sportsmanship is not a matter of what the rules are, but consists in playing by the rules and taking defeat gamely. One unwritten rule is that spectators may properly go quite wild and use violent language. Don't be shocked; it is all in fun! Americans, like the British, admire skill and luck, and they particularly delight in anyone who can "take it" without showing any sign of distress.

Most Americans want more than anything else to settle down and have a home with children in it. But you will have to get used to what they mean by "settling down". It does not mean finding a secure job and a house and stopping there for ever. It means first of all finding a line of work with prospects of higher pay and a "future," rather than security. Love of home, also, is not necessarily connected with a house. Americans move often and may attach their home feeling almost entirely to their furniture and car. This mobile life may make you homesick or it may not. Anyhow, you may as well like it, for this is the way of life that has built the British Commonwealth of Nations as well as the United States. This is how your people have made history, and now it is your turn.

Your social position will be what you and your husband make it. There are different social levels in America and you will get placed in one of them, partly by your husband's job, partly by where you live, and partly by your own personality. Except for a few girls who have connections in America already, most British brides arrive entirely unknown. No one knows who you were at home, and in most places no one cares very much to dig into your past. Practically no Americans are able to "place" you by your accent. It is what you are that is important. If they like you, they like you, and if they don't like you, a good address in London is no help. This, in fact, is what most Americans went to America for—a fresh start with no questions asked.

It is hard to give helpful information on housekeeping because there are so many kinds of homes in America. You may be among that quarter of the population who live on farms, or the other quarter in small towns of 2,500 or less, or you may live in a city. The climate may be anything from that of New England, with snow all winter, to that of New Mexico, which is more like North Africa.

Your income may be small at first, and houses for people with small incomes in America are not Hollywood mansions. However, a girl can save a discouraging-looking house by a first-class job of homemaking at small cost. If you don't know how already, you can learn. Women's magazines are full of good suggestions, and many schools and colleges run evening classes in domestic science. If you live on a farm, be sure to ask about the Home Demonstration Meetings.

As a matter of interest you may like to compare your probable income with the average scales in America. You will notice that the vast majority have to make do on not very much.

17% of all American families receive less than £120 a year.

29.5% of all American families receive from £120 to £250 a year.

35.3% of all American families receive from £250 to £500 a year.

15.8% of all American families receive from £500 to £1,000 a year.

2.1% of all American families receive from £1,000 to £5,000 a year.

0.3% of all American families receive over £5,000 a year.

You may wish to take a job so as to increase your family income. If so, you will not be considered queer, nor will people look down on you. But do not waste your time. In America practically every housewife does her own work. Only people with incomes of $5,000 (about £1,250) or more can afford a full-time maid, though with less money you may be able to get some part-time help. Your main job, therefore, will be running the house. Since your husband's prospects of promotion may be improved by an attractive home, you may add more to the family budget by homemaking than by working for pay, unless you can get a really good job at a good salary.

As your income increases, you should know where to move and what to afford. Working out a family budget is valuable whatever your income may be. You will find that money does not go as far as you might expect, and planning pays. To give you an idea of living costs, here is the budget of a family of four, living in Rochester, a fairly big city north of New York. The family income (pre-war) was $2,400 or £600. Their expenditures were:

	£	s.
Food	175	
House payments and taxes	80	
Fuel and lighting	42	10
Telephone	10	
Instalments on household equipment and fund for upkeep	30	
Clothes	45	
Car (payments and depreciation)	37	10
Health (dentist, doctor and reserve)	30	
Recreation (holidays, cinema, etc.)	35	
Insurance, savings	47	10
Miscellaneous	67	10
	£600	

You will notice an item of £30 for health. In America there is no general health scheme, though locally there are good doctors and health services. Get the name of a good doctor from your relatives or a nearby hospital. Most general hospitals are private, but they usually have clinics to give advice and consultation. They can tell you of the available maternity and child-care services. Take care in choosing your doctor and your children's doctor. There are quacks in all countries.

You will notice, too, the expense for the family car. Most families have cars, running all the way from luxury models down to ancient rattletraps costing about £5. People travel farther than in Britain, to work, to school, to market, and to social affairs, and vacations are often taken at great distances. Travel for two or three people is cheaper by car than by railway.

Another item is household equipment and upkeep. There are all sorts of gadgets and there is terrific advertising pressure to make you think you cannot live without them. Americans have become fairly hardened to this pressure and most of them buy only what they really need to live comfortably. There is still a lot of comfort in having savings in the bank, rather than too many gadgets.

Go as slowly as you can in buying clothes until you know the markets and are familiar with what your friends wear. It usually pays to look for quality and good, simple styles that will last. Bows, "froo-froos," and tricky cuts may look appealing in store windows and prices may seem attractively low, but it is always better to be conservatively smart than flashy.

Incidentally, don't try to outfit yourself on this side of the ocean. You will want to see what kind of climate you will be living in before building up a wardrobe. In New England and the northwest you will need mostly heavy, warm things, with only a few cool dresses for summer. In the South, the proportion will be the reverse. You will also need to experiment, because of central heating. Houses are warm inside, usually around 70°, so Americans dress lightly indoors and put on extra-heavy overcoats when going out into the 20° or lower winter weather. You may find central heating difficult to get used to—but remember Americans like it, so bear it cheerfully. If you buy any clothes before leaving, use up your precious coupons on woollens, as British-made sweaters and tweeds are still of the best in quality and price.

In general, Americans eat three good-sized meals a day, with no regular tea, but often a snack at bedtime.

Breakfasts consist of fresh fruit or fruit juice, cereal (usually cold, with cold milk), eggs and bacon (crisply fried), toast (hot and buttered), and coffee.

Lunch is usually light, if your husband is away at work. In small towns where he can come home it is a family meal and may be called dinner.

Dinner, usually served about 6 o'clock, consists of tomato juice or soup, meat or fish, at least one fresh vegetable and potatoes; often also a salad. "Dessert" is pie, cake, fruit, or ice-cream.

Tinned foods are generally good, but not all equally so. Try various brands and keep track of the names, to find which you like best. No one will think you are a lazy housewife when you use tinned food, if it is good. Frozen foods of many kinds are on the market and are delicious. "Delicatessen" stores sell cooked meats and other foods that may often save the situation when you are rushed or have guests. It is important not to make too much of a fuss about a dinner party: your guests are more interested in you than in an elaborate meal. Better to use the tin-opener than to be hot and flustered.

No matter what your income is, it never pays to try to show off or live beyond your means. You and your husband will be judged not so much by what you spend, as by whether you are pleasant company and seem to be on the way up. Don't think that throwing money around really leads to "good contacts". Most Americans, especially those who may help your husband to get ahead, respect thrift and good management.

Just as in all countries, the American ideal is often higher than common American practice. Americans believe in a friendly attitude to all kinds of people, which they call "being democratic". They often fail to live up to this standard, especially with people who seem "different". Less than half the American people are of British origin, and many of the others, chiefly from the European continent, are not entirely Americanised. There is some unfriendliness between people of different ancestry when they are settled in large groups still recognisable as "foreign". There is prejudice in some areas against Black Americans, in some areas against Jewish communities, in some against Catholics, and in some against Asians, especially Japanese. There is often high feeling connected with politics and labour problems. However, you can remember that the Americans have built up a sincere friendship with the people of Canada, and they are constantly becoming more friendly with the Mexicans. You will find that although there are some groups who don't like the British, among the great majority such prejudice as there is about British girls is in your favour.

In spite of the mixture of peoples and the confusion of a new country, there is a large amount of agreement on the American ideals of freedom and good will. Americans do not like to be "pushed around" any more than British people do. Along with the feeling that everything is "born free and equal" and ought to have an equal chance in life, is a spirit of hope, with great expectations for the future. In spite of many short-comings, America is a new country where past achievements are only a starting-point for the future.

You will be welcome in America, for you, too, have taken your chance and embarked on a great adventure. Americans admire courage. They will wish you good luck and happiness in your new life in the New World.

✎ TRAVEL INFORMATION ✎

These arrangements are subject to alteration

✎ TRAVEL PAPERS ✎

Preliminary application for a visa can be made at any time by post to the Consular Section, American Embassy, I, Grosvenor Square, London, W.1. If you live in Scotland, send your application to the American Consulate at Glasgow, or if in Northern Ireland, to the American Consulate at Belfast. Nothing further needs to be done until you have made up your mind when you want to go. Then you should submit by post the required evidence that you have assured means of support in America. This evidence may be in the following form:

1. Husband's sworn affidavit of support.
   His affidavit should include the following details regarding himself:
   Full name.
   Place and date of birth.
   Nationality.
   Rank or position.
   Salary and allowances.
   Insurances and other financial resources, such as bank deposits, property, etc.
   Whether or not he has any other dependants.

---

2. Letter or statement from husband's Commanding Officer confirming the pertinent information contained in the affidavit.

---

3. If preceding husband to the United States in order to join his relatives, documentary evidence is required from the relatives indicating their willingness and ability to receive applicant into their home.

The Embassy will then advise you in writing that your papers are in order and will tell you to apply to a shipping company for transportation. As soon as you are able to obtain a letter or coupon confirming that accommodation is available, it should be forwarded to the Embassy. Then an appointment will be arranged for a personal interview at the Embassy and for your medical examination. The documents you should bring with you at this time are:

Valid passport:	(British passports and exit permits are issued by the British Passport and Permit Office, 1, Queen Anne's Gate Buildings, Dartmouth Street, London, S.W.1, or Branch Office, Liverpool).
Birth certificate:	two CERTIFIED copies.
Police record:	two copies (not required if you have resided only in the British Isles).
Marriage certificate:	original (which will be returned).
Military or Naval Discharge:	original, if you have served in the Forces (which will be returned).
Photographs:	three (3), on thin paper with light background, two and a half inches square.
Evidence:	showing that upon your arrival in the United States you will have a railroad ticket or enough money to buy one to your final destination.
Visa fee:	$10.00 (at present £2 10s.).

If, in order to obtain a passport, your government requires evidence that an American visa will be issued, a statement to this effect will be furnished after you have made formal application and have qualified for it.

If your papers are in order and if you have not come down with a contagious disease on the ship, you may expect to be allowed to proceed without being detained at Ellis Island.

∽ TRANSPORTATION ∽

It is regretted that because of the severe curtailment of shipping-space available for civilians at the moment, the Embassy is no longer able to assist wives and minor children of American servicemen in obtaining transportation. Consequently, arrangements must be made directly with a shipping company. Shipping companies may refuse to arrange transportation for applicants who are expecting the birth of a child within four months of the proposed date of sailing. The cost of transportation from port of departure to port of arrival in the United States is at present approximately £40, first class, £29, second class, infants, £2 10s. and up, depending on age. It is not possible to foresee travel conditions after the end of the war.

∽ LUGGAGE ∽

Any questions relating to the amount of luggage permitted should be taken up with the appropriate company arranging transportation. Household goods that have been used for a year or more may be taken in duty free. Clothing, jewellery and other personal articles for your own use are free of duty whether new or used.

∽ MONEY ∽

British currency regulations do not permit a traveller to take out more than £10 during wartime. However, for any further information in this connection, application should be made to any bank.

∽ ARMY ALLOTMENTS ∽

Any enquiries regarding allotments or allowances should be addressed to Claims and Allowances Section, U.K. Base, APO 413, U.S. Army.

American citizenship is not acquired through marriage. Application for naturalisation may be made only after arrival in the United States with an immigration visa. A period of three years is required before final citizenship papers are issued, and meanwhile you remain a British subject. The requirements for naturalisation include ability to read and write and some knowledge of American geography and government. There are citizenship courses to prepare candidates for the examination, which is not a very difficult one.

∽ CHILDREN ∽

Generally speaking, the minor child of an American parent has claim to American citizenship and would not require a visa to enter the United States. The birth of the child should be reported to the Citizenship Section of the nearest American Consulate, with a request for an American passport for the child.

✑ FIANCÉES ✑

The documents required for a fiancée of an American serviceman are similar to those applicable in the case of a wife. However, at present it is not the usual practice of the British authorities to grant exit permits to fiancées unless their future husbands are already in the United States.

✑ BRITISH NATIONAL SERVICE ✑

A British subject, although married to an American citizen, is still liable for national service. Enquiries should be addressed to the local office of the Ministry of Labour and National Service. An applicant serving in the Forces should apply to her Commanding Officer about discharge or transfer.

GENERAL

ADAMS, James Truslow
   The Epic of America. Routledge, 1932, 1944. (8s.6d.)
BENET, Stephen Vincent
   America. New York, 1944.
BENTLEY, Phyllis
   This is America. Gollancz. (1s.)
FURNAS, J.C.
   How America Lives. Lane, 1942. (12s. 6d.)
HAZARD, Lucy L. (edited)
   In Search of America. Crowell, 1930.(22s. 6d.)
HUBBELL, J. B. (edited)
   American Life in Literature. Harper, 1936. (26s.)
   (Anthologies of short stories on America.)
LILIENTHAL, David E.
   TVA. Democracy on the March. Penguin Special, 1944.
   (9d.)

REGIONAL

BOYD, James
   Drums. 1936. (Story of the American Revolution.)
CARROLL, Gladys
   As the Earth Turns. Macmillan, 1933. (7s. 6d.)
   (Maine farm through the seasons.)
CATHER, Willa
   My Antonia. Heinemann, 1932. (3s. 6d.) (Bohemian
   settlers in Nebraska.) Death Comes for the Archbishop.
   Heinemann, 1927. (4s. 6d.) (New Mexico, 19th century.)

CHASE, Mary Ellen
    Mary Peters. Collins, 1935. (7s. 6d.) Collins, 1936.
    (3s. 6d.) (Maine seacoast and China trade)
DAVENPORT, Marcia
    The Valley of Decision. Collins, 1944. (12s. 6d.)
    (Pittsburgh steel industry and labour.)
DAY, Clarence
    Life with Father. Chatto & Windus, 1936. (7s. 6d.)
    (Life in New York in the 1880's.)
FERBER, Edna
    Cimarron. Heinemann, 1933. (4s. 6d.) (Settling of
    Oklahoma to the 1920's.)
FISHER, Vardis
    Children of God. Methuen, 1939. (10s. 6d.) (Story of
    the Mormons—Utah.)
HAWTHORNE, Nathaniel
    The Scarlet Letter. Published by various companies.
    House of the Seven Gables. Published by various
    companies. (Stories of New England.)
LEWIS, Sinclair
    Main Street. Cape, 1920. (9s.) (Life in the Middle West.)
MARQUAND, John P.
    Wickford Point. Hale, 1939. (5s.) (Boston family.
    Massachusetts north shore.)
MILLER, Caroline
    Lamb in His Bosom. Muller, 1934. (7s. 6d.) (Georgia.)
MITCHELL, Margaret
    Gone with the Wind. Macmillan, 1938. (12s. 6d.)
    (The South, civil war and reconstruction.
MORLEY, Christopher

Kitty Foyle. Faber & Faber, 1935. (8*s*. 6*d*.)
(Philadelphia, Main Line and white collar girl.)

PAGE, Elizabeth
The Tree of Liberty. Collins, 1940. (9*s*. 6*d*.)
(Revolution to 1806.)

RAWLINGS, Marjorie Kinnan
The Yearling. Heinemann, 1944. (10*s*. 6*d*.) (Florida)

SMITH, Betty
A Tree in the Yard. Heinemann, 1944. (10*s*. 6*d*.)
(Life with a poor Brooklyn family.)

STEINBECK, John
Of Mice and Men. 1937. The Grapes of Wrath.
Heinemann, 1941. (8*s*. 6*d*.) (California migrant workers.)

STONG, Phil
State Fair. Grosset, 1933. (4*s*. 6*d*.) (Iowa.)

SUCKOW, Ruth
The Folks. Grosset, 1936. (6*s*.) (Iowa and the Middle West.)

TARKINGTON, Booth
Alice Adams. Grosset, 1937. (6*s*.) (Middle West, small-town, "average" American family.)

WESCOTT, Glenway
The Grandmothers. 1927. (Wisconsin.)

WISTER, Owen
The Virginian. Grosset, 1929. (6*s*.) (The western cattle country.)

ENGLISH	AMERICAN
All the best	Good luck
Baby specialist	Pediatrician
Bank holiday	Legal holiday
Banknote	Bill
Basin	Mixing bowl
Beer or "Bitter"	Ale or beer
Biscuit, sweet	Cookie
Biscuit, unsweetened	Cracker
Bill (in a restaurant)	Check
Black treacle	Molasses
Blind	Window shade
Block of flats	Apartment house
Boiled sweets	Candy (hard)
Book a table	Reserve a place
Book passage	Get tickets
Booking office	Ticket window
Boots	Shoes
Braces	Suspenders
Bureau	Writing desk or secretary

ENGLISH	AMERICAN
Cab Rank	Taxi stand
Char	Maid
Cheerio	So long
Chemist's	Drug store
Chest of drawers (low)	Bureau
Chesterfield, settee, couch	Davenport, couch, sofa
Chips	French fried potatoes
Cinema	Movies
Cloth overshoes	Galoshes
Cornflour	Corn starch
Corsets	Girdle
Cotton wool	Cotton
Court shoes	Pumps
Cupboard	Closet
Dress circle	Balcony
Dressing table	Dresser
Dust bin	Ash can
Face flannel	Wash rag, wash cloth
First floor	Second floor
Flat	Apartment

ENGLISH	AMERICAN
Fresh butter	Sweet butter
Frying pan	Skillet, frying pan or spider
Galoshes	Rubbers
Geyser	Water heater
Goods wagon	Freight car
Gramophone	Phonograph
Greengrocer	Grocery store
Grilled	Broiled
Ground floor	First floor
Guard	Conductor or brakeman
High boots	Boots
High Street	Main Street
Indian corn (maize)	Corn
Ironmongery	Hardware
Joint	Roast
Jug	Pitcher
Ladder (in stocking)	Run

ENGLISH	AMERICAN
Lavatory	Toilet
Lift	Elevator
Luggage	Baggage
Mackintosh	Raincoat
Made-to-order	Tailor-made
Margarine	Oleomargarine
Marrow	Summer squash
Napkins (baby's)	Diapers
Nursing home	Private hospital
Paraffin	Kerosene
Paraffin wax	Paraffin
Petrol	Gasoline
Plate	Silverware
Post	Mail
Porridge	Oatmeal
Potato crisps	Potato chips
Pram	Baby carriage
Pullover	Sweater

ENGLISH	AMERICAN
Railway	Railroad
Return	Round trip
Scone	Biscuit
Shooting	Hunting
Shop	Store
Shopping	Marketing
Shutter	Blind
Single (ticket)	One way
Snack bar	Lunch counter
Stalls	Orchestra seats
Solicitor or barrister	Lawyer
Stone bottle	Jug
Stores (household)	Groceries
Subway	Underpass
Suspender belt	Garter belt
Suspenders or sock suspenders	Garters
Sweet (at lunch or dinner), savoury	Dessert
Sweets	Candy
Tap	Faucet
Threepenny and sixpenny store	Five and ten

ENGLISH	AMERICAN
Tinned	Canned
Tram	Street car
Tramp	Bum (slang)
Trousers	Pants
Trunk call	Long distance
Tube	Subway
Undercut (of beef)	Tenderloin
Upper circle	Second balcony
Valve (wireless)	Tube
Verandah	Porch
Vest (man's)	Undershirt
Waistcoat	Vest
Wire	Telegram
Wireless	Radio

∞ TABLE OF CURRENCY ∞

BRITISH		AMERICAN	
¼d.	=	½ cent.	No coin
½d.	=	1 cent.	Copper
1d.	=	2 cents.	No coin
3d.	=	5 cents.	Nickel
6d.	=	10 cents.	Silver
1s.	=	20 cents.	No coin
2s.	=	40 cents.	No coin
2s. 6d.	=	50 cents.	Silver
5s.	=	$1.00	Paper or silver
10s.	=	$2.00	Paper
£1	=	$4.00	No currency
£5	=	$20.00	Paper

AMERICAN		BRITISH	
Cent (penny)	=	½d.	
Nickel (5 c.)	=	3d.	
Dime (10 c.)	=	6d.	
Quarter (25 c.)	=	1s. 3d.	No coin
Half-dollar (50 c.)	=	2s. 6d.	
Silver dollar	=	5s.	
Dollar bill	=	5s.	
$2 bill	=	10s.	
$5 bill	=	25s.	No currency
$10 bill	=	50s.	No currency
$20 bill	=	£5	
£5	=	$20.00	Paper

*The following stories, features and poems were
published in Good Housekeeping during the war years.
At times poignant and sometimes amusing, they convey the
special relationship between the British and Americans.
Perfect reading material for a British war bride awaiting
her ship to America.*

∽ WE'RE GLAD TO MEET YOU MRS AMERICA! ∽

SEPTEMBER 1941

*This article describes the life and
characteristics of four American women.
A charming and useful read for any
British bride leaving for her new
life in America.*

∽ WE'RE GLAD TO MEET YOU
MRS AMERICA! ∽
By Jane Marshall

Jane Marshall introduces some American women who share in the battle for democracy!

We all hope that Anglo-American co-operation is going to be one of the features of the world after the war, as it has been during it. The Americans speak our language, their ideals are fundamentally the same as ours. But do we really know the Americans?

The trouble is that, though we know the vast size of the United States, many of us cannot grasp it. The geography books tell us that the basin of the Mississippi alone would hold all Western and Central Europe. But in the atlas the United States appears on a page the same size as that devoted to England, and it is very easy to think of the different states as if they were English counties, instead of tremendous stretches of country.

Among the many Americans in this country to-day, helping us with our war effort, are four women with whom I have talked. Two of them are young, two middle-aged. Their backgrounds vary from the hamlets of New England and the forests of Minnesota to Georgia's cotton-fields and the megalopolis of New York. The difference between them may help to give us some idea of the various types that make up American womanhood to-day, may help us to shed some of our generalisations about Americans.

48

Mrs. G. comes from Maine, in the north-east of New England. In appearance she is like the older pictures our artists used to draw of Americans, before they got the idea that all U.S. citizens wore horn-rimmed glasses and chewed gum. She has high cheekbones, an aquiline nose and a long jaw. She has the complexion so typical of many middle-aged American women, not as pink-and-white as ours, but with a smooth glow. She has shrewd, kindly eyes, a prim New England voice, and a manner which is dignified without being standoffish.

At home Mrs. G. lives in a cottage on the estate now owned by her brother. Though small, this estate has been in the family ever since they settled there in Mayflower days, and the nearby town bears the family name. This type of family is the nearest we shall find in the U.S.A. to our own squirearchy, but it is less feudal, more neighbourly, in its relations to the people round about.

At the outbreak of war President Roosevelt told his people that no one expected them to remain neutral in thought. Long before America began to give us active aid, the general sympathies of the country were with us, for America was built on the ideas of freedom, and it was freedom and democracy which the emigrants of all lands sought when they crossed the seas. But in New England there is more than that. There is a genuine feeling of kinship between them and ourselves. Their surnames, their place-names, are in many cases the same as ours. Their way of living, the culture which they have cherished, is the same as ours.

Mrs. G. stands for New England. Upright, generous, rather old-fashioned, perhaps, in the sense of clinging to old values and old traditions. Certainly she and her type have little in common with the film America of gangsters, blondes and wild parties.

From Maine to the south, to Georgia. Mrs. F., like Mrs. G., is middle-aged. She is small, dark and plump, slower in speech and movement than her northern sister, with the drawling southern voice which is regarded as the most beautiful of American enunciations. She too looks back to traditions. They are based, not on small communities of hard-working emigrants, but on wide estates, on the culture of the Southern families, where all the women were beautiful, all the men gallant, where hospitality was sacred and an insult meant a duel.

Since the civil war (in which Mrs. F.'s ancestors fought those of Mrs. G.) much of this life is dead. Mrs. F.'s life now is more like that lived by people in our own country towns. But it still moves slowly, with the lazy rhythm of the South.

"What do I do back home? Why, I cain't jus' say." The story as she eventually told it sounded very much like the life of many English women—the house, the garden, shopping expeditions and bridge parties, except that I think American women like to be lectured to more than we do. Mrs. F. spoke with great enthusiasm of some of the "fine, interesting Europeans" who had come to give lectures in her home town.

"No, we're not very interested in local politics. It's always been the idea that the southern girl doesn't mix herself up with that sort of thing—leaves it to the men. Perhaps," she added with a smile, "that's why things aren't just as well done as they might be in our part."

Mrs. F. is here on Red Cross work, and very hard

work it is, too.

"After all," she said deprecatingly, 'anything to do with nursing is a woman's job. I didn't say we were brought up to do nothing in Georgia. We're with you alright, even if we don't hustle quite as much as the Yankees!"

Then there is Miss H., young America this time, for she is only twenty-three. And sophisticated America, because she is a New Yorker, and has lived all her life among the speed and cosmopolitan atmosphere of that city. It is difficult to define exactly what it is about her appearance that stamps her as an American, perhaps it is those high cheekbones again, and the way that the face tapers down from a broad forehead to a pointed chin. Possibly it is the long-legged grace of her movements—for no one can combine so well the art of moving with ease, with yet a faint suggestion of coltishness, as your American girl.

Daughter of a well-known public man, Miss H. might be described in terms of our "Society" girl. But she is not content to spend her time at parties or sporting events. She has all young America's urge to get things done.

"What's the point of women making a place for themselves on equal terms with men if they don't do something with it?"

To Miss H. and her contemporaries the question so often debated in magazines here, of "career versus marriage" is nonsense. They take it for granted that an intelligent woman will be able to make a success of both.

"The girls I meet over here seem surprised that I'm a College girl. Why, over in the States all girls like me go to College. There's a wide scope for study, and you can take almost any subject you like. One of my friends took child psychology and now helps in a clinic—though she *is* married. I took economics myself."

They want to learn these young women. They do not like the idea of being useless in this modern world. They have not, perhaps, the old feudal sense of personal responsibility, but they have a strong sense of social responsibility. Good times they may have, but they are not "good-time girls."

New Yorkers are cosmopolitan, but these women realise well enough what Hitlerism would mean to the civilisation they have built up, and they are doing what they can help to smash it.

In thirty-year-old Mrs. M., the fourth woman, you feel at once that dynamic charm which is so typical of American women. She gives the impression of being always on her toes, always interested. Smart, groomed as American girls always manage to be, you feel behind the sophistication the gusto with which a young nation sees the world.

But although she represents the American professional woman she comes from a background difficult to envisage. Her home is Minnesota, the middle-west state whose northern boundary adjoins Canada. This state was by-passed by the pioneers who trekked westward during the nineteenth century, and was late in development.

By the time Mrs. M. was born though, the district had jumped in one bound from wildness to modernity. For all their amazing switch over to modern life, there is still a lot of the pioneer atmosphere left among these folk. "That's why the women are so powerful in the towns. Pioneer women are very important. They represent civilisation. So what they ask for they have to get. I guess that's why everything is made as good as possible for the kids."

These people are full of local patriotism. Every townsman is a good citizen, very anxious to make a fine showing with his town. This spirit has been laughed at, and it sometimes produces rather comic results. But on the whole it is a fine and healthy outlook, and one from which we ourselves could well learn. They look to the future not the past.

Well, there they are, these four ordinary American women, typical of countless thousands "back home." They are important not only for the work they are doing, but for the impressions they are creating all the time. More than any amount of articles or books or radio talks, these women give the lie to ignorant and one-sided generalisations about their countryfolk. They help, too, to show how solid a basis there is for future co-operation between our countries. Even where we differ, we can still admire—their directness, their outspoken sincerity, that fresh, eager outlook, due perhaps to being born into a young country, their poise and perfect grooming, are all very charming and attractive. Hail America!

✐ WOMAN AND WAR ✐

JUNE 1941

*A poem describing the heartache
and burden of war.*

❧ WOMAN AND WAR ❧

The woman has to live after the war:
This is her burden, this her pride and sorrow.
To-day is mercifully swift, but on the morrow
Who knows what heartache waits? The future more
Than present holds a woman's hopes and fears.
For her no easy—"Let to-morrow dawn,
Bring what it may!" Her children greet that morn,
And she must face it too. Those after-years,
Those are her question. Will this be the last,
The final throw of force? Or will her sons,
Ignoring all the lessons of the past,
Fall once again a sacrifice to guns?
This is the woman's burden, this her sorrow—
Man lives to-day, but woman lives to-morrow.

G.M. Chaplin

JUNE 1944

An amusing story of two homesick American soldiers looking for romance in England.

∽ A PLACE TO SIT ∽
By Margaret Pulsford

*They weren't fresh . . . just a couple of nice
lads who felt a bit homesick and very thirsty!*

Red walked up the hill with Shorty. The sun beat down on
the white chalk road, roughened and gutted by the rain-
storms of years. Coarse grass grew at the sides of the road,
and there were a great many loose pebbles and lumps of
chalk.

"What the hell did we come for, anyway?" Red asked.

"May as well see as much as we can while we're here,"
Shorty said.

Neither of the men looked at the other as he spoke. They
knew each other too well. Red had a round, youthful face that
should have been pleasant, but with the heat and irritation
and also the disappointment that had been growing in him
for weeks, he looked surly. He was tall, with a lean, boney
frame.

Shorty was lightly built, with pale, fine-drawn features. He
moved with the nimble paces of the city-bred, and the
nickname he had acquired in the Army was inevitable. The
only similarity between the two was the uniform of an
American private.

"I'm dry," Red said after a while, and looked up at the sky,
his face puckered and disgruntled.

"Aw," said Shorty, "quit grousing."

Red passed a big hand across his mouth. "And I thought
it was never hot in England," he said.

Shorty did not answer directly, but sent his glance towards the top of the hill.

"Pretty nice-looking houses up there," he said, "maybe if we called in, they'd give us a drink or something."

Red laughed. "Quit kidding, they'd probably yell for the cops."

"Aw," Shorty said, "there are some pretty nice people about."

"Where? Tell me that, will you?"

"You're sore," Shorty said.

"Yeah, I've got smallpox and didn't know it. We've all got smallpox."

"You shouldn't try giving dames a rush," Shorty said.

"Why not?" Red asked. "What's the matter with me?"

"You're an American."

"My God," Red said, "that makes me as good as anybody else and a darn sight better, if you ask me."

"I keep telling you," Shorty said patiently, "you're a stranger. Folks don't understand."

"To hell," said Red.

They went on walking up the hill, leaving behind them the flat fields only broken with the long, shallow arches of the furrows. The air was so still it seemed to cling to their faces, wrapping their heads in the heat.

Shorty stopped and searched for his handkerchief. "Sure is hot," he said.

"You're telling me," said Red. "The only thing that'd cool me off now is an English dame. That's all I want. That's all I need. An English dame on ice."

"Jeeze," said Shorty, "they're not all on ice."

"Show me one that isn't," Red demanded.

"How'd you make out with Nellie Pollock?" Shorty asked and grinned.

"She was no good," Red replied and looked away. "There are dames like that any place, I guess. I want a girl who is somebody. Someone I can call my girl, see?"

"Sure," said Shorty, who also wanted a girl.

The hill began to grow steeper.

"What'd you choose this place for, anyway?" Red asked.

"The Downs are at the top," said Shorty. "I had a yen to see the Downs."

"Downs!" said Red. "What the hell are Downs, anyway? Don't make sense. Nothing in this country makes sense, if you ask me."

"You're a small-town boy," Shorty said. "That's your trouble."

"Cade is a small town, isn't it?" Red demanded angrily. "But it might be a desert, the Sahara or something."

"Cade isn't a real small town. It isn't in the country for a start."

"Well, whatever it is, people could speak to a guy, couldn't they?"

"Sure, but give 'em time. We've only been here seven weeks, and in camp most of the time."

"Seven weeks and nobody's said a word to us, scarcely," Red said. "All they do is look at you in that way they have, or the girls start acting as if you've insulted them. Insult a girl! Me!" All his young chivalry was outraged.

"You've behaved like a sap from the start," said Shorty,

who knew exactly which incidents Red was recalling in his hurt mind. Before he had begun to make a name for himself as a commercial artist, Shorty had worked as a clerk in an English club in New York and was convinced he knew all the aspects of the British character. Moreover, he was more patient than Red, with that quality of wary approach to people which comes from being poor in a big city.

But Red had always lived in a small town where he'd known everybody, and he didn't understand reserve. He'd come to England loaded with the vitality that made him friends and customers at home in his job as salesman, and with no doubt whatever that there wasn't another soldier in the American army more capable of waking up the British. He'd show 'em! Screwy old England!

But nothing had gone right. The rout he had suffered during their first off-duty hours, soon after they'd landed, still rankled. They'd gone to the Crown and Feathers because it was the oldest inn in the district. It lay about a mile and a half beyond the town, and for this reason few soldiers reached it. As they pushed through the door, they'd seen at a glance there were no other Americans there. The silent, dusty atmosphere, smelling of burning logs and beer, the sight of the sleepy British, stolidly drinking, had been too much for Red. This was funny old England as he'd imagined it, just waiting to be pepped up by America. So he'd wisecracked and shown off, with Shorty as his embarrassed foil. Nobody had taken any notice, nobody had given any indication of either hearing or seeing, yet as he left, Red knew that all eyes followed them and that those eyes were laughing.

"Hell," he said to Shorty outside. What are we, lepers?"

"Americans," said Shorty philosophically. "What'd I tell you? No good trying to bust in like that."

"I'd like to bust 'em all on the snoot," said Red, thus expressing his hurt feelings. "I only wanted to be friendly. Give 'em a laugh."

Red wanted a girl. So did Shorty. But they had no luck in Cade, a suburban growth on the outskirts of a prim and somewhat smugly respectable coastal town, which prided itself on the niceness of its district .When they tried to get into conversation with the kind of girls they would have known at home, they were either snubbed outright, or treated with an elusive courtesy equally barren of results.

"You can't blame 'em," Shorty said. "They've got their own fellows to think about. Besides, some of our boys have cut up rough, and maybe they're scared."

"Can't they see when a guy's on the level?" Red asked forlornly.

So it was very dull in Cade for Red and Shorty, as for most of the thousand-odd other young Americans in the camp— dull and chilling. Yet, as Red often observed, there were houses, rows of them, nice-looking places, and people living in them like their own folks back home, people with sons of their own. Why didn't they open their doors and give a fellow a break? More than girls, they wanted to be asked into a home. And nobody had asked them. This to Red was evidence that the British had no heart whatever.

And it wasn't as if Red hadn't tried to make friends. He'd learned his lesson from the Crown and Feathers. He'd been quieter, but it hadn't done any good, not even when he'd bought drinks. They bought drinks back, but they went away like strangers and, if he saw them again, likely as not they didn't seem to recognise him.

In despair he'd picked up Nellie Pollock, a big, slovenly girl with peroxided hair. He'd known she was no good. Once when he was on the street with her, he'd heard a girl say to another: "I don't know where these Yanks get such awful women."

He'd wanted to overtake the girl and say, "Lady, it's because girls like you are so darn snooty!" But the courage to do so was not in him. He hadn't seen Nellie Pollock again, and he was glad there was never anything of consequence between them. But the loneliness and boredom had begun once more.

And last night he'd got into another mess. He was thinking about this bitterly as they went on and a dog came out of a hedge and began to bark at them.

"Look at that," Red said, "even the dogs don't like us."

"Why should anybody like us?" Shorty said. "They've hardly got around to knowing we're here."

"Back home everybody would've known," Red said.

"In your one-eyed town, perhaps," Shorty said. "But in a big one like New York you wouldn't have made a ripple, even if you'd dressed yourself in the Stars and Stripes, even if you'd hung a ticket around your neck saying, 'lonesome.'"

"Who wants to live in New York anyway?" Red asked, resenting the reflection on his home town.

"It's a good place once you know it, same as any other place, I guess," Shorty said. "I wouldn't mind walking up Broadway right now. Gee, I wouldn't mind any part of New York. Guess I'm homesick."

"You're homesick! I'd give a year's pay to walk into Willie's drug store on Main and hear ole Mac say: 'What's yours, a maple with whipped cream?' Gee, I could do something to a maple special."

"Maybe somebody'll give us a cup of tea if we go knock on a door," said Shorty, who felt unexpectedly choked in the throat.

"Who?"

"Someone, maybe. We'll just ask," Shorty said, thinking hungrily that it would be pretty swell to sit in somebody's parlour in a real home. He kept his face turned away from Red, afraid lest he was showing just how much he was wanting this.

"And you say a thing like that after last night," Red said.

As they walked on, the dog that had barked at them now followed them. He walked beside Red, wagging his tail.

"'Lo, fellah," said Red and held out his hand.

The dog crouched, flattening his head and snarling. Then it dashed away. Red watched it disappear into a hedge. Snakes, you could never tell with the British, not even the dogs!

Pursuing this line of thought, his mind returned to the events of the night before, when they'd gone to a dance in the big industrial town in the hope of making friends.

"How did I know she wouldn't like being called gorgeous?" he asked Shorty.

"English girls are different," Shorty said.

"They sure are," Red agreed bitterly. "Back home a girl thinks there's something wrong if you don't call her beautiful. Besides, I'd had a dance with her."

"Listen," Shorty said. "Get wise to yourself. You need more than one dance before you can start calling English girls gorgeous when they're the right kind. And they all were, at that joint."

"Sure, and that was why we bought the tickets," Red said. "We wanted to get to know a couple of nice girls, didn't we? And she asked me to dance. I didn't do anything."

"She was a hostess, you dope. Besides, you sang to her," Shorty accused.

"I've got a nice voice," Red said, and grinned.

"That's what you think. But maybe she didn't like it. Anyway, if you had to sing to her, why didn't you do it on the dance floor, and not in the bar with your arm around her? You must have seen she didn't like it."

"Heck," said Red, "I just thought she was a little shy, perhaps, or putting on an act."

"You put on the act," Shorty declared, "playing around like Cæsar Romero. And then you said, 'Let me take you home, honey. You're what I've been looking for.' "

"Well, she was," said Red, who had a simple and literal mind. "Besides, I thought if I got to know her people, we'd be in."

"And we were out," Shorty said. "If she'd found a loudspeaker, it couldn't have got around quicker that we were just another pair of fresh Americans."

"They certainly took their cold shoulders out of storage," Red agreed, morosely.

At last they reached the summit of the hill. The scene was very beautiful. The Downs that had been hidden now showed with one great rise leading to another. The sun edged those that were farthest away with light, an edging as sensitive as the outline of a lip. From the ground rose the sweet, honeyed fragrance of gorse.

For a moment neither of them spoke. Then Red said: "Guess this is the English countryside you read about. Guess there's nothing quite the same. And it's so small." His mind, as he spoke, was comparing the gentle landscape with the huge wheatfields he had seen once on a trip to the western states, so huge that when the wind passed over them it made the heads of the wheat move like the waves of a limitless ocean.

"These are the Downs," said Shorty with satisfaction. After all, he'd found them. He'd brought Red out to them. In his memory he was seeing Sixth Avenue in New York. When he was small his parents had an apartment on Sixth. The windows were so near the railway known as the "L" that the people in the trains could look in and see exactly what his family were doing.

"They don't look so small to me," he said, his eyes delighting in the wide-flung, misty view, as he remembered the pressure of people, the thunder of traffic, the grey closeness of brick he had always known. "Did I ever tell you my folks came from somewhere near these parts—my grandparents. I can remember the ole man quite clearly. He was always talking about the Downs.

"You don't say," said Red.

"Sure," said Shorty. "I've got English blood in my veins." He would not have confessed under torture the queer pleasure it gave him to say this. He was American, a hundred per cent. American. Yet looking across the tender rise and fall of the hills, he began to wonder if anybody was a hundred per cent anything. We're all much the same, he thought, all off the same block, all human beings.

"Where'd your folk come from, Red?" he asked unexpectedly.

"Scotland. Three generations back," said Red, and saw that his feet were in heather. "Plenty of this stuff in Scotland," he said, shuffling one foot into the springing purple flowers, pleased at the recollection. Somehow it gave him a link that was comforting.

"Sure," said Shorty, who understood.

Red undid another button of his tunic and licked his lips. "Sure could do with a coke," he said.

Shorty looked about him. "There are plenty of houses," he said, "let's try one. They might be pleased, at that. We could explain we came up here to look at the Downs. Anyway, we'd get a drink of water."

"Not likely!" said Red. "I don't want to get the bird again. We'd only annoy 'em, Shorty. They just don't like us."

"You feel low," Shorty said.

"I sure do. I wish we'd been sent out East instead of here. Yet I always wanted to come to Britain." He sat down on the short turf, his face disconsolate and moist with heat. Shorty sat down beside him and pulled out a package of cigarettes. They began to smoke, looking across at the hills and then towards the houses, with their red-tiled roofs and encircling gardens.

Suddenly Red raised his head. "Here comes a dame," he whispered and looked painstakingly at the hills ahead.

"Well, have you come up here to see the view?" a voice

asked. "It's the finest in the county. What do you think of it?"

Red did not move, but Shorty got to his feet.

"It's a grand view," he said.

"You boys look hot." This unexpected observation so amazed Red that he turned his head and smiled at the woman, who wore a grey printed dress that suited her grey hair.

"I'm just going home. Come along back with me and I'll give you a cup of tea, or a glass of beer, if you'd prefer it."

"Gee, thanks, mam," said Red, and rose with embarrassed awkwardness.

"My name's Adela Marsh, Mrs. Marsh," said the grey-haired woman.

"He's Robert Wilson and I'm Mark Welsh," said Shorty.

She gave them tea in the garden with freshly picked raspberries. "There's only milk and very little sugar," Mrs. Marsh said, "but you must make the best of it!"

"Everything's swell," said Shorty. "Why, mam, you're the first person in the whole of England who has ever asked us home. We appreciate it a whole lot."

"That sounds as if you're homesick?"

Shorty and Red nodded.

"I'm sorry," Mrs. Marsh said. "But we do what we can, and there are so many Americans, and our own boys as well. And rations are so tight—it's very difficult."

"But Mrs. Marsh," Red said, "we don't expect anything, but we'd sure like to sit in a real home once in a while, feeling as if folks wanted us." His young, puzzled eyes looked at her.

"You've been thinking we're inhospitable," Mrs. Marsh accused with a smile.

"Not that, exactly," said Red hastily. "A lot of our fellows have a swell time. They get asked to big houses for parties. Maybe we've just been unlucky. And, anyway, we don't want grand parties so much as getting to know people, our sort of people. It gets lonesome."

Mrs. Marsh nodded. "I know, but we're a funny lot. The people you mean belong to the middle class and we're the most difficult of any to know. You see, we're proud, and while some of us would like to do more, we're afraid we haven't enough to give you. And some of us just don't know how to break the ice. Then again, often you Americans, you know, . . ." Her eyes twinkled as she spoke. "Well, some of you are a bit high-spirited, to say the least, and we're not used to it. You think it's going to bring us out of our shell, but it only pushes us farther in."

Shorty looked at Red. "What'd I tell you?"

But Red's eyes were turned towards the house. A girl was coming through the long French windows, a girl with warm brown hair and a smiling mouth. She was dressed in slacks and shirt.

"You're late, Kathleen," Mrs. Marsh said.

"I've been having a bath, darling," Kathleen replied. "I've been cleaning out Mrs. Moll's rabbit hutches all the afternoon. The poor old girl's as blind as a bat."

"My daughter, Kathleen," said Mrs. Marsh, as Red and Shorty stood up.

"These boys are feeling homesick. I hope they'll come and see us again," Mrs. Marsh explained.

"We'd sure like to," said Shorty.

"How long have you been over here, and where are you

71

stationed?" Kathleen asked.

"Seven weeks, and we're near Cade," replied Red, who had not felt so happy for a long time.

"Ugh. Awful spot!" said Kathleen. "And how are you getting on with the insular British?"

Red and Shorty grinned shyly. At last Shorty said: "We haven't had much of a chance to find out."

Kathleen laughed. "You're saying we're difficult to know! We certainly are. We had to live here three years before we knew anybody, and then they weren't sure of us."

"Do you mean you're the same to each other as you are . . ." Red floundered. "Well, to anybody from another country?"

Kathleen laughed. "Worse, if anything," she said.

"Isn't it the same everywhere, except in the really country places or among the very rich, who all seem to know one another, anyway?" Mrs. Marsh said. "I once went to New York when I was much younger, and found it difficult to get to know my own kind of people there, at first. Yet out in rural districts I had the time of my life. People in towns are always much more cautious."

"That's what I've tried to tell Red," Shorty said, beaming. "But he can't get the idea. Give people time, any place, and they'll loosen up. But some need more time than others. Like the British."

"It beats me," said Red. "So it's not because you don't like us?" He appealed to Kathleen.

Kathleen considered, and Red felt his spirits fall. If this girl didn't like him, it would be too much.

"You mean, do we like Americans? You might just as well say, do Americans like us! But it's all a matter of

72

understanding each other's characteristics. Until we do, the barriers are up. Most Americans are easy to know. Most of us aren't. We both take pride in being the way we are, and that's why we frequently ruffle each other."

"Say, that's sense," Shorty said, impressed.

"I'm a bright girl," Kathleen remarked.

"And nobody could accuse you of being modest," said her mother.

"Ticked off again," said Kathleen cheerfully and stood up. "I've got to go back to Mrs. Moll." Red and Shorty got up as well.

"We must get back to camp," Red said. "Can we come part of the way with you?"

"Of course," Kathleen said. "Mrs. Moll's house is on the way to the station."

They set off. The sun was still high and the air hot. But neither Red nor Shorty noticed.

"It was swell of your mother to ask us in, like that," Red said.

"I'm glad she did," Kathleen told him. "It's rotten to be lonely. I hated it when we first came here. I didn't think we'd ever make any friends. I hated everybody. But now I know stacks of people, and they're all just as nice as those I left behind when we came south. I suppose there's not much difference in people really, once you know them."

"Guess that's right, too," said Red, who, four hours ago, thought nothing of the sort.

They parted at the door of Mrs. Moll's little cottage, and Red asked, "Can we really come and see you again?"

"Of course, we want you to come," Kathleen said.

"Perhaps my sister'll be home next time. Anyway, I'll get some friends and we'll have a party."

"That'll be wonderful," Red said.

Kathleen watched them as they walked away down the hill, and when they reached the bend and turned around to catch a last glimpse of her, she waved to them.

As they went on Red said, "Say, it's like being home again, having someone wave to you."

Shorty smiled. "What'd I tell you? You've got to get to know folks, then you're home, wherever you are. The British are no different from us, not in the things that matter."

"Guess that's so," Red agreed, "and my, she's a swell girl, isn't she? Do you think she liked me?"

"Sure she liked you," said Shorty. "That's why I'm so darn glad she's got a sister!"

❦ A SOLDIER'S HONEYMOON ❦

JUNE 1944

*A soldier longs for his honeymoon
and a happy home.*

∽ A SOLDIER'S HONEYMOON ∽

Some day soon. . . . Our Home!
With white gate and crocus-studded lawn;
A workshop and a vice to make a bookcase;
A kitchen for the heirloom sample "God is Love."
A parlour with a floral couch
And dad's piano from the storage room,
Surmounted by our wedding group.
A job with cash enough to spend on Opera.
Our Home—and you.

What say you, my love?

Some day soon. . . . Our Home!
With tiny slippers in the nursery
And scarlet pantaloons,
And Donald Duck gazing with saucer eyes
On innocence—so delicate, like shell china.
Good neighbours and a garden
With bronze chrysanthemums.
Our Home—and you.

. . . The bridal chamber door swung open.
On the threshold stood a young warrior
In armour, smiling.

Speak, my friend!

I am To-morrow.
I passed this way and saw your dreams
Drifting out, like singing clouds.
You talk of Peace, but when the church bells ring—
'Twill be my call to arms.
More blood, more toil, more tears,
Are all I offer.
I have your home, your nursery, your floral couch,
Stored in your Future's vaults,
But I am still To-morrow.
The battle is not won until, with gory arms,
All three of us can march victorious
Through the shining portals
Of To-day!

Coleman Milton

⮾ SET THE WILD ECHOES FLYING ⮾

JULY 1944

*This extract tells the tragic story of
an American soldier stationed
in Scotland – he falls in love with a
young ticket-seller at the local cinema.*

✎ SET THE WILD ECHOES FLYING ✎
By James Street

The story of a wild and gallant Irish-American,
by a favourite American author

Cleburne was not a good soldier in the eyes of his comrades. He had a habit of doing things his own way, and it often worked. He never drew a bead as the other recruits did, but he usually hit the target, and that annoyed his instructor.

The first flare-up between him and his fellows came when he suggested that the stock of his rifle was too short. "I want to notch my stock," he explained.

"Notch it?" a soldier demanded.

"Uh huh. You know, cut a notch every time I kill a German."

The men were disgusted with this "Yankee" boasting. Then they laughed, scornfully, and began to shun him. The recruiting sergeant returned to the line just to watch him.

The spiritual depression, the Mississippi blues, came back to Cleburne, and he was moody and sullen until he chanced one night to step out of the black-out and into a cinema. The ticket-seller smiled at him, a professional smile that she gave all customers.

In time to come, the townspeople would gossip about how it started. Well, the smile started it. The beginning was as simple as that.

Cleburne's mouth flew open and he gaped at the girl, for never before had a strange girl smiled at him. He sort of stumbled into the cinema and saw an American western. It was an America that he had never seen, or anyone else, but, in a way, it looked something like home; the dusty roads and the unpainted shacks. It was the happiest evening he had spent in a long time and, naturally enough, he associated that film with home and the girl with that film. Man's mind is not a complicated thing.

As he left the cinema, he walked slowly by the booking-office, glancing at the girl. He noticed that she had long hands and they worked expertly as she made change. He didn't notice then (and he never did) that her hands were large at the knuckles. He didn't notice that she smiled at all the customers. She had brown hair, just plain brown hair. But to him it looked golden.

Cleburne never remembered returning to his barracks, and then he couldn't sleep. The next night he was back at the cinema, and the next and the next.

The sergeant, realising something was amiss, followed him one night and was standing just beyond earshot when she spoke her first words to Cleburne. After all, a ticket-seller will eventually recognise a customer. She said, "You haven't missed an evening here for a week or so."

"I like movies," said Cleburne.

"Oh, you are an American."

"Yes'm."

She gave her attention to another patron, and Cleburne went in, but the sergeant went back to the barracks and told what he had seen. "He has gone balmy over Fannie Moore. You know Fannie? Down at the cinema."

"Fannie's a smart girl," said one of the soldiers. "That Yank won't fool her. Besides, he looks like a gorilla."

That was the night they decided to call Cleburne's bluff, to prove that he was a liar, and to put him in his place. When he returned, they gathered around and the sergeant said, "Listen, Yank, about that big farm you say you own. . . ."

"It ain't but fifty acres of farm land," said Cleburne. "The other land is in timber."

"Nevertheless, that's too much land for one man to own."

Cleburne looked from one face to the other and didn't understand.

"And another thing. About this battle you keep talking about. There hasn't been any battle in America. America's not even in the war."

Cleburne laughed out loud then, the first time any of them had ever heard him laugh. I wasn't talking about this war, you pecker-woods!"

"There wasn't any battle in America in the last war," the sergeant persisted, and the men nodded approval.

"You lugs are crazy as betsy bugs. Franklin was a battle fought in Tennessee in '64. 1864."

"That long ago!" The men were bewildered. "Then how could you have been there?"

"I wasn't there. Grandpa was." He just shook his head and walked away in disgust.

"I told you he was balmy," the sergeant said. "Whoever heard of worrying about a battle fought *that* long ago."

The next day the regiment went down into England, thence to France and eventually to Dunkirk. Cleburne was rescued without having fired a shot. As he and the sergeant waded into the surf and tumbled into a boat, Cleburne looked back at the beach and said, "We charged 'em at

Franklin. We charged 'em six times."

The sergeant was bitter. "You weren't anchored back there. You could have charged." He stared at the burning town, then began laughing hysterically. Cleburne laughed, too. Delirious men do strange things.

The regiment was sent back to the North of Scotland, back to training. All passes were cancelled and the men were confined to their barracks at night. They were too busy during the day and too tired at night even to guy Cleburne. Eventually, the outfit was brought back to its peak and Cleburne's unit was given town leave. He dressed in his best, tried to plaster down his unruly hair and hurried into the cinema.

But she wasn't there. His simple mind conjectured all kinds of things. Perhaps she was dead. Perhaps she was married and gone away. He walked up the street and into the nearest pub. It was filled with soldiers and girls and noise. He went to a corner, found a table and began drinking, paying no mind to the crowd.

The sergeant saw him and was ready for some fun. "Ay, Yank," he said. "I forgot to ask you. Did you notch your rifle at Dunkirk?"

Some of his comrades laughed. Cleburne said, "Get the hell and go away, you buss-eyed apes!"

"How're you going to explain to your grandfather? How many times did he notch his rifle at Franklin?"

Cleburne was staring at the table. "He didn't have a rifle at Franklin. He piped for Pat Cleburne. I have his piob mor at home. Pretty handy with it myself." He said it simply, more as though he were talking to himself.

"A pipe!" The sergeant guffawed. Then he looked around at some of his cronies and they nodded. The sergeant walked to the far end of the room, where one of the regimental pipers was drinking with a crowd. He borrowed the piper's instrument and, holding it aloft, walked back to Cleburne. The crowd was suddenly quiet and watched.

"Now play it," the sergeant said. "Play it, Yank. Or hereafter keep your mouth shut."

Cleburne's first impulse was to grab the sergeant and bump his head against the table, but he realised that would mean trouble. So he took the bagpipe and ran his fingers over the chanter. His second impulse was to play an Irish march, maybe "Leaving Glen Urquhart." But that might bring an argument, and he was in no mood for arguments. So he decided to play "Break Jaw-bone." Then he looked around and that's when he saw her. She was standing by the piper and was smiling at him, for she had recognised him. Cleburne's heavy eyebrows went up, then together, and his pulse began pounding.

"Go on. Play." The sergeant was leaning on the table.

Cleburne tried, but only a wild squeak came out of the chanter and a rumbling bass out of the drones. He tried again, but he couldn't even remember the melody. He was looking at her, and his mind was confused.

The sergeant said, "Is that the way your grandfather piped at Franklin? Small wonder that your side lost." He snatched the pipe and gave it back to its owner, and the crowd laughed again.

She didn't laugh, however. She walked over to him and

said, "I am glad you got back all right. I haven't seen you at the cinema."

"I was down there to-night, but you weren't there." He was surprised at himself, for he was just as calm as you please.

"No, I got off to-night." She sat down and began munching some soggy potato chips. "Can you really play the pipes?"

"Yes'm. Gen'ly. I don't know what happened."

She thought she did, and she smiled again. "What part of America do you live in?"

"Mississippi."

"Oh. I have a cousin in Minnesota. Edward Moore. They call him Ted. My name is Frances Moore. They call me Fannie. Do you happen to know my cousin?"

"No'm." He didn't try to tell her just how far it is from Mississippi to Minnesota, for then it didn't seem so far.

"What's it like where you live?"

"It's river country. A big river and black land. I've got fifty acres of farm land. The cotton ought to be 'way up by now."

"All that land?"

"That ain't much land, Miss Moore. That's just a little old piddling farm. But if I push it, I can get plum' near a bale to the acre. Good corn land, too. If we get a dry spell."

She didn't understand what he was talking about, but she understood him and let him walk home with her. In fact, she even hinted that she wanted him to escort her home. Otherwise, he might have done nothing about it. She had never been anywhere except where she was. She had strange notions of America.

The next time he got leave he went to the cinema and saw

the film twice through, waiting for her to get off. It happened time and again after that. The story that he, with Yankee impetuosity, swept her off her feet, is gossip and nothing more. The only time he ever touched her was the night he took her arm and helped her down some steps.

She knew when the regiment was ready to move out again. He had only a few minutes, so he went to the cinema and stood by her booth. A serial was showing and he said, "I'd rightly like to see this episode. Hate to miss it."

"I'll write you what happens," she said. "I write to several of the boys. To cheer them up."

"I'd be mighty proud to hear from you, Miss Moore." He just looked at her and she looked at him. They didn't even shake hands. "I'll be seeing you," he said, and went back to his barracks.

They sailed first to North Africa, thence to Greece and there they retreated again, before Cleburne had a chance even to bring his gun to his shoulder. In Crete, they were actually advancing and then got an order to fall back again. The men didn't understand it. The stolid Scots took it philosophically, but Cleburne's hot Southern blood was boiling, and he got surly. One of his fellows happened to try to tease him then, and Cleburne knocked him down and paid the penalty.

Back in Africa again, he got the letter. The sergeant brought it to him. Cleburne read it and then went off by himself and read it again. The sergeant told a soldier, "You'd think that was the first letter he ever got."

It was.

She told him about the serial.

He wrote to her that night. It took him two hours to write four pages, and when the letter was finished, he was sweating. The next letter told him that "Riders of the Purple Sage" was showing at the cinema. In the third one, she said that she was writing to him so often that she didn't have time to write to anyone else. "We are showing a picture about the Mississippi River," she wrote. "It's beautiful. I would like so to see that country."

It took eight pages for him to tell her that he wanted her to see it with him. And thereafter she signed her letters, "With love, Fannie."

The regiment, having recovered from its retreats, was finally ordered into the desert. Cleburne hated the desert. "I like big rivers," he said. "This stuff gets me down."

The Germans were on the rampage again and the regiment had scarcely reached the front before the army was ordered to retreat into Egypt. Cleburne found the major near a water truck and said, "Sir, I'm tired of running."

"So are we all," the major said curtly.

"I don't aim to run no more," Cleburne said. "I ain't even drawn a bead yet. Not a frazzlin' one."

The major wiped his mouth with the back of his hand. "You will," he said. "We will cover the retreat. By this time to-morrow we will be fighting right about here."

"You mean we're going to take on the whole army?"

"We are going to try to slow them down." He actually seemed light-hearted, for he smiled at the American, the first time he had smiled at him since Cleburne enlisted. "Were you outnumbered at Franklin?"

"We were always outnumbered. But not this bad." He started away, kicking the sand as he walked.

"Oh, Mulvaney. Just one thing. Most of us won't be here to-morrow night."

"That was sort of bothering me." Cleburne took off his helmet and ran his heavy hand through his hair. "Do me a favour, sir."

"What is it?"

"I own a little bit of land back home. And a couple of mules and a house. If I don't get back I don't know who'll get it. Can you fix it up so it'll go to a friend of mine? 'Cause I ain't aiming to run no more."

"Yes, we can fix that."

The Mississippi farmer marched in front of the men. He swung his pipe to and fro to get the beat, then began swirling the march; a Southern Irish piper playing the song the other side sang at Franklin. A Yankee song. That's what Cleburne thought—he didn't know that the melody was taken from an old Southern hymn, "O brothers, will you meet us upon Canaan's happy shore?"

The men watched his march back and forth. One man moved, and then they all got up and, without orders, fixed their bayonets at the assault and followed him.

The enemy was caught off balance. Then they opened fire with small arms. Cleburne had his head tilted and was swirling for the men to follow him when the mortar shell exploded at his feet. He held his pipe in one hand and gripped his stomach with the other. The sergeant glanced at him, then hurried by. The force of the explosion hurled him backwards. He struggled to his feet and, in trying to move forward, he began stumbling. Instinctively, he ran, trying to regain his balance. He didn't know what he was doing. He didn't know anything from the time of the explosion until he pitched forward within fifty yards of the German lines.

The sergeant swore that he hurled himself into the lines. "And I heard him shout 'Charge 'em again.' It took twenty Jerries to cut him down."

Actually, Cleburne didn't say a word from the time he started piping until he was killed.

When the Eighth Army moved out, rolling westward, the sergeant saw to it that the story was told. "He used to borrow my gun rag," the sergeant told an Englishman.

"I saw him roll some enormous boulders into a pile," said another. "With his bare hands."

"I saw him rip a Bren off a carrier and kill a hundred Jerries," said the sergeant. "And what do you think of little Fannie Moore? He left her rich and she's going to America. . . ."

The English passed the tale along. Fannie Moore, a little Scottish Cinderella, had inherited a thousand acres on a river that's five miles wide.

✑ WELCOME, BRIDES! ✑

JULY 1945

*This delightful editorial from
Good Housekeeping welcomes foreign
war brides to Britain.*

✍ WELCOME, BRIDES! ✍
By *Good Housekeeping*

Recently it was the happy privilege of *Good Housekeeping* magazine to produce, in co-operation with the Office of War Information of the U.S.A., a booklet entitled *"A Bride's Guide to the U.S.A."* This little work was designed to smooth the path of those British girls who, during the War, married Americans.

The enthusiastic reception given to this Guide, on both sides of the Atlantic, set us thinking about those other brides who soon, we hope, will be coming to these islands from overseas to make their home here. Perhaps they, too, will be in need of friendly "tips" on how things are done here, and the best way to approach the problems of housekeeping in a strange land.

This country is still in the grip of shortages and controls. Transport is difficult, and it will often not be possible for the husbands and relations of our new British citizens to meet and take them home. That, added to our customary shyness and reserve, may sometimes make our welcome appear less warm than it is in reality. But, Brides from Overseas, from our own Dominions, from our great Allies, the U.S.A., Russia, France, Belgium and the rest, be assured that we are genuinely happy to have you with us and of us.

We know that all readers of *Good Housekeeping* will do all in their power to help the Overseas Brides coming to their communities to feel wanted and at home. If relatives-to-be will inform their friends of the coming of the new member of the family, it will be possible to give a real neighbourly welcome, and to arrange those little informal parties that do so much to make a stranger feel at home.

And when the first round of festivities is over, it is to mothers- and sisters-in-law that will fall the friendly duty of making the new bride a real member of the family. Ask her into your kitchens, get her to show you her ways of cooking, as well as initiating her into British housekeeping methods. If she has any problems that you cannot solve, write to us at *Good Housekeeping*—or encourage her to write herself if she's shy of telling you all her difficulties. The Institute will be happy to help in running the new home, in marketing and cooking, while our other experts are there to be consulted on etiquette, dress, cosmetic fashions, or indeed on any point. We shall deem it a privilege to do all we can to help her.

CREDITS

Project Editor: Carly Madden
Design Manager: Gemma Wilson
Designer and Illustrator: Abby Franklin
Senior Production Controller: Morna McPherson